D0561352

mother's little book
of home-baked treats

mother's little book
of home-baked treats

RYLAND
PETERS
& SMALL

LONDON NEW YORK

Senior Designer Iona Hoyle

Editor Ellen Parnavelas

Production Laura Grundy

Art Director Leslie Harrington

Editorial Director Julia Charles

First published in the UK in 2012
by Ryland Peters & Small
20–21 Jockey's Fields
London WC1R 4BW
and in the US
by Ryland Peters & Small, Inc.
519 Broadway, 5th Floor
New York, NY 10012

www.rylandpeters.com

The recipes in this book have been published
previously by Ryland Peters & Small.

10 9 8 7 6 5 4 3 2 1

Text © Tonia George, Linda Collister, Annie Rigg,
Susannah Blake, Sarah Randell, Hannah Miles,
Isidora Popovic and Ryland Peters & Small 2012

Design and photographs
© Ryland Peters & Small 2012

ISBN: 978 1 84975 195 7

A CIP record for this book is available from the
British Library.

US Library of Congress cataloging-in-publication
data has been applied for.

Printed in China

Notes

• All spoon measurements are level unless
otherwise stated.

• All eggs are medium, unless otherwise
specified. It is generally recommended that
free-range eggs be used. Drinks containing
raw or partially cooked egg should not be
served to the very young, very old, anyone
with a compromised immune system, or
pregnant women.

• Ovens should be preheated to the specific
temperatures. Recipes in this book were tested
using a regular oven. If using a fan-assisted oven,
follow the manufacturer's instructions for
adjusting temperatures.

contents

baked with love

Whether it's an indulgent layer cake for an afternoon tea party, some sticky buns to add to a breakfast tray or a pretty box of cookies to give as a gift, this beautiful little book is packed with delicious recipes, gathered together to help honour and celebrate mothers everywhere.

Nothing beats a homemade cake fresh from the oven and this little book is packed with sweet delights for all the family to enjoy. Featuring pretty-as-a-picture bakes such as exploding berry crumble muffins, delicate rosewater cupcakes, almond praline macarons and victoria sponge cake with fresh mint & strawberries, these recipes can be used by home bakers everywhere to make delicious treats for every occasion.

Mother's little book of homemade treats is the perfect gift for mother or for any daughter or son who wishes to make this Mother's Day unforgettable.

pecan & maple syrup sticky buns

250 ml/1 cup whole milk, plus extra for glazing

85 g/6 tablespoons butter

500 g/4 cups strong white plain/all-purpose flour

50 g/¼ cup packed light brown soft sugar

7 g/¼ oz. easy-blend dried yeast

½ teaspoon salt

1 egg, beaten

filling

75 g/5 tablespoons butter, softened

75 ml/scant ⅓ cup maple syrup

75 g/⅓ cup packed light brown soft sugar

1 tablespoon ground cinnamon

100 g/1 cup chopped pecan nuts

makes about 16

These deliciously sticky buns are best served warm on the day they are made, so if you are eating them after that, warm them a little in the oven before serving.

Put the milk and butter in a saucepan and heat gently until the butter has melted. Remove from the heat and leave to cool until blood temperature. Put the flour, sugar, yeast and salt in a large bowl.

Pour the egg into the cooled milk and beat. Make a well in the centre of the dry ingredients and pour in the milk mixture. Gradually draw in the floury mixture with a wooden spoon until it is all combined. Bring the dough together with your hands, then tip out onto a lightly floured work surface and knead for 10 minutes, until smooth and the dough springs back when poked. Place in a lightly oiled bowl and cover with plastic wrap. Leave to rise for 1–2 hours.

Meanwhile, to make the filling, mix the butter, maple syrup, sugar and cinnamon in a small bowl and set aside. Push the air out of the dough and lay it on the work surface. Using the heel of your hand, flatten and shape it into a rectangle about 30 x 40 cm/12 x 16 in. Spread the filling over the surface of the dough. With one of the long sides facing you, roll up the dough like a Swiss/jelly roll and chill in the fridge for 1 hour.

Cut the roll into 2-cm/¾-in slices. Arrange these, flat side down, on a baking sheet spaced about 2 cm/¾ in apart so that they have room to expand. Cover loosely with plastic wrap and leave to rise for 30 minutes, until puffy. Meanwhile, preheat the oven to 200°C (400°F) Gas 6.

Brush the buns with milk and slide into the oven. Immediately reduce the heat to 180°C (350°F) Gas 4 and bake for 12–15 minutes, until cooked through and golden.

breakfast bakes

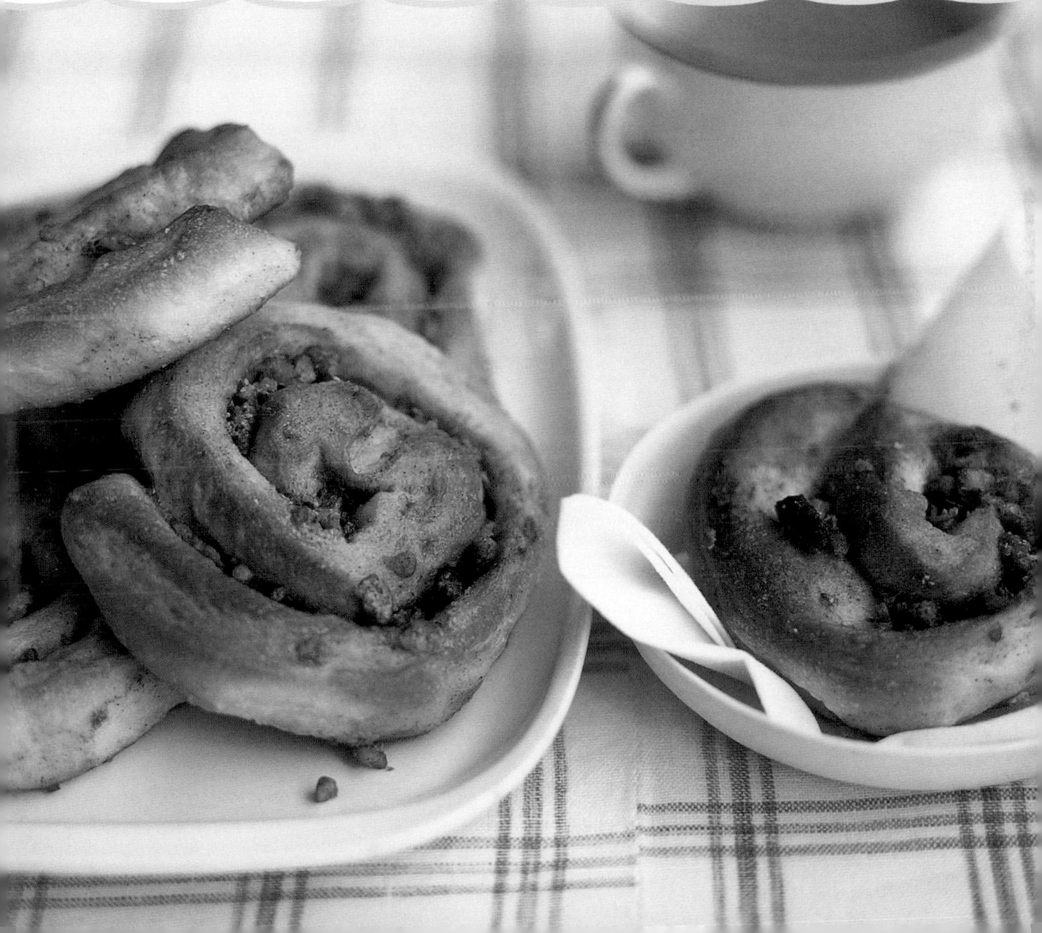

summer fruit & white chocolate muffins

These very moist muffins are packed full of fruit and nuggets of white chocolate. They are the perfect treat with a mid-morning coffee.

2 eggs

80 g/¼ cup plus
2 tablespoons unrefined
(caster) sugar

50 ml/3 generous tablespoons
vegetable oil

a few drops of vanilla extract

150 g/1 cup plus
2 tablespoons plain/
all-purpose flour

1½ teaspoons baking powder

1 large nectarine, pitted
and sliced

70 g/⅔ cup hulled and
quartered strawberries

70 g/2½ oz white
chocolate, chopped

topping

1 nectarine, pitted and sliced

60 g/½ cup raspberries

30 g/¼ cup hulled and
quartered strawberries

packed light brown soft sugar,
to sprinkle

*a muffin pan, lined with
6 large muffin cases*

makes 6

Preheat the oven to 180°C (350°F) Gas 4.

Put the eggs, sugar, oil and vanilla in a mixing bowl and mix well until you have a smooth liquid. Mix the flour and baking powder together in a separate bowl, then mix into the wet ingredients. Stir in the nectarines, strawberries and white chocolate until evenly mixed.

Fill each muffin case about two-thirds full with batter. Scatter the fruit for the topping over the muffins and finish with a sprinkling of sugar. Bake in the oven for about 25 minutes. Do not be tempted to open the oven door halfway through baking as it might cause the muffins to sink. When they are ready, they should be well risen and springy to the touch.

Muffins are always best eaten warm from the oven, but if you have some left over you can refresh them with a quick flash in the microwave. Store in an airtight container for 2–3 days.

blueberry pancakes

Perfect blueberry pancakes should be light and fluffy, with a good rise on them. The secret is to use some water – an all-milk batter makes the pancakes heavier.

125 g/1 cup self-raising/
rising flour

1 teaspoon baking powder

2 tablespoons granulated
sugar

¼ teaspoon salt

1 egg

100 ml/⅓ cup whole milk

50 g/3½ tablespoons butter,
melted

150 g/1½ cups blueberries,
plus extra to serve

maple syrup, to serve

serves 4

Preheat the oven to low.

Sift the flour and baking powder into a large mixing bowl and stir in the sugar and salt. Put the egg, milk and 75 ml/scant ⅓ cup water in a jug/pitcher and beat to combine.

Stir half the butter into the wet ingredients in the jug/pitcher. Mix the wet ingredients with the dry ingredients until no lumps of flour remain. Wipe a heavy-based frying pan with a scrunched-up paper towel dipped in the remaining melted butter. Heat up, then drop in 4 tablespoons of the batter. Cook for 1–2 minutes on the first side, then scatter over a few of the blueberries and flip the pancake over. Cook for 2 minutes, until golden and cooked through. Keep warm in the oven while you make the rest.

Serve with more blueberries and plenty of maple syrup.

exploding berry crumble muffins

375 g/3 cups plain/
all-purpose flour

3 teaspoons baking powder

1 teaspoon bicarbonate of
soda/baking soda

150 g/¾ cup unrefined
(caster) sugar

½ teaspoon salt

2 eggs, beaten

115 g/1 stick butter, melted

200 g/¾ cup sour cream

60 ml/¼ cup whole milk

180 g/1½ cups raspberries

topping

100 g/¾ cup plain/
all purpose flour

75 g/⅓ cup butter, chilled
and cubed

2 tablespoons unrefined
(caster) sugar

30 g/⅕ cup flaked almonds

a 12-hole muffin pan

makes 12

These look like the muffins sold in cafés which seem to have exploded with their generous proportions. There is no secret trick to this – just fill the muffin cases to the top.

Preheat the oven to 170°C (375°F) Gas 3. Line the muffin pan with paper cases and grease the surface of the pan where the muffins will rise and stick.

To make the topping, put the flour and butter in a food processor and pulse briefly, just until the butter is blended. Tip out into a bowl and add the sugar and almonds, pressing the mixture together with your hands.

To make the muffins, sift the flour, baking powder, bicarbonate of soda/baking soda, sugar and salt into a large mixing bowl. Put the eggs in a small jug/pitcher, add the melted butter, sour cream and milk and whisk to combine. Pour the wet ingredients into the dry ingredients and scatter the raspberries on top. Using a large spoon, fold until the mixture is moistened. It needs to be lumpy and shouldn't be overworked otherwise the baked muffins will be tough.

Spoon into the paper cases right to the top. Finish by scattering over the topping. Bake in the preheated oven for 25–28 minutes for large muffins, or 18–22 minutes for the smaller ones. Leave to cool for 5 minutes in the pan before transferring to a wire rack.

blueberry lime friands

If you haven't come across friands before, you will soon be converted. Based on the French financier, they are small, light-textured cakes and very moreish. If you don't want to invest in a special friand pan, you can make these in a regular muffin pan.

125 g/1 stick butter

75 g/½ cup shelled, blanched whole hazelnuts

125 g/scant 1 cup icing/confectioners' sugar

100 g/¾ cup plain/ all-purpose flour

finely grated zest of 2 limes

175 g/1¾ cups blueberries

4 large egg whites

lime syrup

freshly squeezed juice of 1 small lime

40 g/¼ cup caster/ superfine sugar

a 9-hole friand pan, well buttered

makes 9

Preheat the oven to 200°C (400°F) Gas 6.

Melt the butter in a small pan and leave to cool slightly.

Whiz the hazelnuts in a blender until finely ground.

Sift the icing/confectioners' sugar and flour into a large mixing bowl. Stir in the ground hazelnuts, lime zest and blueberries.

Put the egg whites in a large, scrupulously clean bowl and whisk until they form soft peaks.

Using a large metal spoon, fold half the egg whites into the flour mixture with half the melted butter – be as gentle as you can be. Fold in the other half of the egg whites and melted butter.

Divide the mixture between the holes of the prepared friand pan. Bake in the preheated oven for 20 minutes.

To make the lime syrup, heat the lime juice and sugar together in a small saucepan, stirring, until all the sugar has dissolved.

Leave the cooked friands to cool for 5 minutes, then make a few holes in the top of each one using the point of a small, sharp knife. Carefully drizzle a little of the lime syrup over each of the warm cakes, allowing it to seep into the holes. Leave the friands in the pan until completely cold, before running a knife around the edges and turning them out.

fig & hazelnut breakfast bread

500 g/3¾ cups strong white bread flour

2 teaspoons fine sea salt

50 g/¼ cup granulated/caster sugar

7-g/¼-oz. package fast-action dried yeast

2 tablespoons hazelnut oil

200 ml/¾ cup hand-hot water

2 tablespoons blanched hazelnuts, toasted and chopped

300 g/2 cups ready-to-eat dried figs, quartered

2 baking sheets, oiled

makes 2 small loaves

This bread is delicious toasted for breakfast. Rather than spreading it with butter, try serving it with a generous helping of soft cream cheese.

Sift the flour and salt into a large bowl and stir in the sugar. Add the yeast and stir again. Pour in the hazelnut oil and enough hand-hot water to make a soft but not sticky dough. Add the hazelnuts and figs and knead well to combine.

Turn the dough out onto a lightly floured work surface and knead for 5–10 minutes. Divide into two rough loaves and put on the prepared baking sheets. Leave to rise in a warm place for about 1 hour, or until the dough has doubled in size.

Preheat the oven to 220°C (425°F) Gas 7.

Cut a couple of slashes in the top of each loaf and bake for about 25–30 minutes, until golden and firm and the bases sound hollow when tapped. Cool on a wire rack.

Eat on the same day or let cool completely, wrap in foil and freeze. When you remove the bread from the freezer, thaw it completely and wrap in foil, then reheat for 5 minutes in a hot oven.

sugary doughnut muffins

75 ml/scant ⅓ cup
sunflower oil

150 g/scant ½ cup plain
yogurt

½ teaspoon vanilla extract

2 large eggs, beaten

275 g/2 cups plus 2
tablespoons self-raising/
rising flour

½ teaspoon bicarbonate
of soda/baking soda

a pinch of salt

100 g/½ cup caster/
granulated sugar

75 g/⅕ cup blueberry
jam/jelly

topping

25 g/2 tablespoons unsalted
butter, melted

50 g/¼ cup caster/
superfine sugar

*a 6-hole muffin pan,
lined with paper cases*

makes 6

*This is a recipe for anyone who likes a sugary doughnut
but dislikes the deep frying involved in making them.*

Preheat the oven to 190°C (375°F) Gas 5.

Put the oil, yogurt, vanilla extract and eggs in a bowl and beat together.

In another large bowl, mix together the flour, bicarbonate of soda/baking
soda, salt and sugar. Pour the wet ingredients into the dry ingredients and
mix until just combined. It needs to be quite lumpy but make sure there are
no floury pockets left in the mixture.

Drop 1 generous tablespoon of the batter into each paper case. Make a dip
in the mixture and spoon in a generous teaspoon of the jam/jelly. Divide
the remaining batter between the paper cases to cover the jam/jelly. Bake
in the preheated oven for 18–20 minutes, until well risen. Set aside, still
in the pan, to cool for 5 minutes before you apply the topping.

When the muffins have cooled for 5 minutes, brush their tops with the
melted butter for the topping and roll in the sugar. Transfer to a wire rack
to cool to room temperature.

love hearts gingerbread

basic spiced gingerbread

2 tablespoons golden/corn syrup

1 large egg yolk

200 g/1²/₃ cups plain/all-purpose flour, plus extra for dusting

½ teaspoon baking powder

1½ teaspoons ground ginger

1 teaspoon ground cinnamon

¼ teaspoon ground nutmeg

a pinch of salt

100 g/7 tablespoons butter, chilled and diced

75 g/⅓ cup packed light brown soft sugar

plain/all-purpose flour, for rolling out

icing

500 g/3¾ cups royal icing sugar/mix

75–100 ml/⅓–½ cup cold water

pink food colouring paste

heart cutters in assorted sizes

baking sheets, lined with non-stick parchment paper

disposable piping bags

small star-shaped piping nozzle/tip

makes 10–12

Why not give a box of these cookies to your mother on Mother's Day to let her know how much she means to you?

To make the gingerbread beat together the syrup and egg yolk in a small bowl. Sift the flour, baking powder, spices and salt into a mixing bowl and add the butter. Rub the butter into the flour mixture with your fingertips. When the mixture starts to look like sand, add the sugar and mix with your fingers to incorporate. Add the egg-yolk mixture and mix with a wooden spoon until starting to clump together. Tip the mixture out onto a lightly floured surface and knead gently to bring together into a ball. Flatten the dough into a disc, wrap in plastic wrap and chill for 1–2 hours. Preheat the oven to 170°C (325°F) Gas 3.

Lightly dust a clean, dry surface with flour and roll the dough evenly to a thickness of 2–3 mm/ ⅛ in. Use the cutters to stamp out as many cookies as possible, re-rolling and stamping until all the dough is used. Arrange the cookies on the prepared baking sheets. Bake the gingerbread in batches for

10–12 minutes or until firm and browned at the edges and let cool completely.

To prepare the icing for piping outlines or details onto the cookies, tip the royal icing sugar/mix into a mixing bowl and add the water gradually, mixing with a whisk until smooth and thick enough that it will hold a ribbon trail when the whisk is lifted from the bowl. To tint the icing, divide it into separate bowls, one for each colour. Using a cocktail stick, add dots of food colouring paste and mix well. Repeat until you achieve the desired shade. Fill the appropriate number of piping bags with this icing. Carefully pipe a fine outline around the edge of each cookie and leave to dry for at least 10 minutes. Add more water to the remaining icing to make it the consistency of double/ heavy cream and spoon into a piping bag. Flood each outlined cookie with icing. Using the thicker icing, pipe more details on the cookies as desired.

blueberry & vanilla macarons

basic macarons
200 g/1½ cups icing/
confectioners' sugar

100 g/²⁄₃ cup ground almonds

120–125 g/½ cup egg whites

a pinch of salt

40 g/3 tablespoons caster/
superfine sugar

purple food colouring paste

purple sugar sprinkles

vanilla cream
250 ml/1 cup double/heavy
cream

1 teaspoon vanilla extract

icing/confectioners' sugar,
to taste

blueberry filling
300 g/3 cups blueberries

1 tablespoon granulated sugar

*2 solid baking sheets, lined
with parchment paper*

*a piping bag, fitted with a
star-shaped nozzle/tip*

*a piping bag, fitted with a
1-cm/½-in nozzle/tip*

makes about 20

*Try filling these beautiful macarons with blueberry purée,
fresh blueberries and a delicate vanilla-infused cream.*

To prepare the macarons, tip the icing/confectioners' sugar and almonds into the bowl of a food processor and blend for 30 seconds. Set aside. Tip the egg whites into a clean and dry bowl. Add the salt and, using an electric handheld whisk, beat until they will just hold a stiff peak. Continue to whisk at medium speed while adding the caster/superfine sugar a teaspoonful at a time. Mix well between each addition. The mixture should be thick, white and glossy. Add any food colouring paste you are using. Dip a cocktail stick into the paste and stir well to combine. Scrape down the sides of the bowl with a spatula.

Using a large metal spoon, fold the sugar and almond mixture into the egg whites until thoroughly incorporated and smooth. When it is ready, it should drop from the spoon in a smooth molten mass. Pipe 6-cm/2½-in-long fingers onto the prepared baking sheets. Tap the baking sheets on the work surface,

then top with sugar sprinkles. Leave the macarons to rest for 15 minutes–1 hour.

Preheat the oven to 170°C (325°F) Gas 3. Bake the macarons on the middle shelf of the oven, one sheet at a time, for 10 minutes. Leave to cool on the baking sheets.

To make the vanilla cream, whip the cream until it will hold soft peaks and fold in the icing/confectioners' sugar and vanilla.

To make the blueberry filling, tip half the blueberries, sugar and 1 tablespoon water into a saucepan and cook over medium heat until the berries soften and burst. Cook until reduced and thickened to a jam/jelly-like consistency. Press through a sieve/strainer into a bowl and leave to cool.

Spread the filling over half the macaron shells and arrange the whole blueberries on top. Pipe vanilla cream between the blueberries and top with the remaining shells.

basic macarons

200 g/1½ cups icing/
confectioners' sugar

100 g/²/3 cup ground almonds

120–125 g/½ cup egg whites
(about 3 eggs)

a pinch of salt

40 g/3 tablespoons caster/
superfine sugar

1 teaspoon vanilla extract

red liquid food colouring

white chocolate ganache

150 g/5 oz. white chocolate,
finely chopped

5 tablespoons double/heavy
cream

1 teaspoon vanilla extract

200 g/1½ cups raspberries

*2 solid baking sheets,
lined with baking parchment*

a clean toothbrush

*a piping bag, fitted with a
star-shaped nozzle/tip*

*a piping bag, fitted with
a 1-cm/½-in nozzle/tip*

makes about 20

white chocolate
& raspberry macarons

*Lightly dip the bristles of a clean toothbrush into liquid food
colouring. Using your fingertips, 'flick' the bristles over
uncooked macarons for a pretty Jackson Pollock effect.*

Prepare the Basic Macarons according to the recipe on page 24, this time piping into rounds instead of fingers and adding the vanilla extract to the meringue mixture instead of the food colouring.

Pipe rounds of mixture onto the prepared baking sheets. Tap the baking sheets sharply on the work surface. Trickle a little red food colouring onto a saucer, then dip the clean toothbrush into it. Flick the bristles over the macarons so that they are flecked with red. Leave the macarons to rest for 15 minutes–1 hour.

Preheat the oven to 170°C (325°F) Gas 3.

Bake the macarons on the middle shelf of the oven, one sheet at a time, for 10 minutes. Leave to cool on the baking sheet.

To make the white chocolate ganache, put the chocolate in a heatproof bowl. Put the cream and vanilla extract in a small saucepan and heat until the cream has come to the boil. Pour the hot cream over the chopped chocolate and leave to melt for 1 minute. Stir until smooth then leave to cool. Cover and refrigerate until thickened.

Fill the piping bag with the white chocolate ganache and pipe 4 rosettes near the edge of half the macaron shells. Place a raspberry between each rosette and sandwich with the remaining macaron shells.

150 g/1 stick plus 2 tablespoons butter, softened

150 g/³⁄₄ cup caster/granulated sugar

2 eggs, beaten

150 g/1 cup plus 2 tablespoons plain/all-purpose flour

2 teaspoons baking powder

3–4 tablespoons milk, at room temperature

50 g/¹⁄₃ cup ground almonds

finely grated zest and freshly squeezed juice of ¹⁄₂ a lemon

2 tablespoons lemon curd

to decorate

1 tablespoon sieved/strained apricot jam/jelly, warmed

100 g/3¹⁄₂ oz. natural marzipan

500 g/1 lb 2 oz. fondant icing/confectioners' sugar

freshly squeezed juice of 1 lemon

food colouring paste in colours of your choice

150 g/1 cup royal icing sugar/mix

tiny sugar flowers

20-cm/8-in square baking pan, greased and base-lined with parchment paper

a small piping bag, fitted with a fine writing nozzle/tip

makes 12–16

fondant fancies

These little cakes are enough for just a couple of mouthfuls and look beautiful iced in contrasting delicate colours.

The day before you want to serve the fondant fancies, preheat the oven to 180°C (350°F) Gas 4.

Cream together the butter and sugar until light and creamy in the bowl of a freestanding mixer. Gradually add the beaten eggs, mixing well between each addition and scraping down the sides of the mixing bowl from time to time.

Sift together the flour and baking powder and add to the mixture in alternate batches with the milk. Fold in the almonds, lemon zest and juice and stir until smooth.

Spoon the batter into the prepared baking pan. Spread level and bake on the middle shelf of the oven for about 25 minutes. Remove from the oven and leave to cool in the pan for 5–10 minutes before turning out onto a wire rack to cool.

The next day, split the cake in half horizontally using a long, serrated knife. Spread the lemon curd over the bottom layer and sandwich the 2 layers back together. Brush the

warmed apricot jam/jelly over the top of the cake. Lightly dust a work surface with icing/confectioners' sugar. Roll out the marzipan to a square the same size as the cake, using the cake pan as a guide. Lay the marzipan on top of the jam/jelly and smooth the surface. Trim the sides of the cake and then cut into neat, 4-cm/¹⁄₂-in cubes.

Mix the fondant icing/confectioners' sugar with enough lemon juice to make a smooth, thick icing to coat the cakes.

Tint the icing with food colouring of your choice by very gradually adding the food colouring. Hold each cake on a fork over the bowl and drizzle the icing over the top and sides to coat evenly. Transfer the cakes to a wire rack and leave for at least 1 hour until set.Whisk together the royal icing sugar/mix and water until thick enough to pipe. Spoon the icing into the piping bag and use to decorate each cake as desired. Top with tiny sugar flowers.

petits fours

50 g/^{1}/$_2$ cup dried sour cherries, roughly chopped, or raisins

2 tablespoons brandy, sweet sherry, or Marsala

125 g/4 oz. dark/bittersweet chocolate, chopped

75 g/5 tablespoons butter, diced

125 g/^{1}/$_2$ cup plus 2 tablespoons granulated sugar

2 eggs

^{1}/$_2$ teaspoon vanilla extract

50 g/^{1}/$_3$ cup plain/all-purpose flour

a pinch of salt

chocolate ganache

75 g/2^1/$_2$ oz. dark/bittersweet chocolate, finely chopped

75 ml/^{1}/$_3$ cup double/heavy cream

^{1}/$_2$ tablespoon packed light brown soft sugar

a pinch of salt

crystallized roses and violets, candied ginger, candied orange peel, silver and gold dragees

a 17-cm/6^1/$_2$-in square baking pan, greased and lined with greased parchment paper

a piping bag, fitted with a star nozzle/tip

makes 25–36

Present these delicious bite-size brownies in place of the usual box of chocolates.

Tip the cherries into a small saucepan, add the brandy and warm gently over low heat. Remove from the heat and leave to cool and soak for 15 minutes.

Preheat the oven to 170°C (325°F) Gas 3.

Put the chocolate and butter in a heatproof bowl and set over a saucepan of barely-simmering water. Stir until smooth and combined. Leave to cool slightly.

Put the sugar and eggs in a mixing bowl and whisk until thick and pale. Add the vanilla and the cherries with any remaining brandy. Sift in the flour and salt and fold until incorporated.

Pour the mixture into the prepared baking pan, spread level and bake on the middle shelf of the preheated oven for 15 minutes.

Remove from the oven and leave to cool completely in the pan, then refrigerate, still in the pan, until the brownies are firm.

To make the chocolate ganache, tip the chocolate into a heatproof bowl. Heat the cream and sugar in a small saucepan until the sugar has dissolved and the cream is just boiling. Add the salt. Pour it over the chopped chocolate and leave to melt. Stir until smooth, then leave to cool and thicken slightly before spooning into a prepared piping bag.

Tip the firm brownies onto a board and cut into about 25–36 cubes. Pipe chocolate ganache rosettes on top of each cube. Top with your choice of decoration and refrigerate until ready to serve.

lavender cupcakes

These delicate cupcakes are deliciously simple with an understated elegance – perfect for serving with afternoon tea.

115 g/¹/₂ cup plus
1 tablespoon caster/
granulated sugar

¹/₄ teaspoon dried lavender
flowers

115 g/8 tablespoons butter,
at room temperature

2 eggs

115 g/³/₄ cup plus
1 tablespoon self-raising/
rising flour

2 tablespoons milk

to decorate

185 g/1¹/₃ cups icing/
confectioners' sugar, sifted

1 egg white

lilac food colouring

12 sprigs of fresh lavender

*a 12-hole muffin pan, lined
with paper cupcake cases*

makes 12

Preheat the oven to 180°C (350°F) Gas 4.

Put the sugar and lavender flowers in a food processor and process briefly to combine. Tip the lavender sugar into a bowl with the butter and beat together until pale and fluffy.

Beat the eggs into the butter mixture, one at a time, then sift in the flour and fold in. Stir in the milk, then spoon the mixture into the paper cases. Bake in the preheated oven for about 18 minutes until risen and golden and a skewer inserted in the centre comes out clean, then transfer to a wire rack to cool.

To decorate, gradually beat the icing/confectioners' sugar into the egg white in a bowl, then add a few drops of food colouring and stir to achieve a lavender-coloured icing. Spoon the icing over the cakes, then top each one with a sprig of fresh lavender. Leave to set before serving.

buttermilk cakes

180 g/1½ sticks butter, softened

200 g/1 cup granulated sugar

2 whole eggs and 1 egg yolk, beaten

1 teaspoon vanilla extract

225 g/1¾ cups plain/all-purpose flour

1 teaspoon baking powder

½ teaspoon bicarbonate of soda/baking soda

125 ml/½ cup buttermilk

meringue buttercream

200g/1 cup sugar

3 egg whites

230 g/2 sticks butter, softened and chopped

1 teaspoon vanilla extract

3–4 tablespoons sieved/strained strawberry jam/jelly

assorted summer berries

icing/confectioners' sugar, for dusting

1–2 muffin pans, lined with paper cupcake cases

makes 12–16

summer berry cupcakes

Topped with a cascade of summer berries and a swirl of strawberry-scented, delicate pink buttercream, these cupcakes are the height of sophistication.

Preheat the oven to 180°C (350°F) Gas 4.

To make the buttermilk cake mixture cream together the butter and sugar until light and creamy. Gradually add the beaten eggs, mixing well between each addition and scraping down the side of the mixing bowl from time to time. Add the vanilla.

Sift together the flour, baking powder, and bicarbonate of soda/baking soda and add to the mixture in alternate batches with the buttermilk.

Mix until smooth. Divide the mixture between the paper cupcake cases, filling them two-thirds full, and bake on the middle shelf of the oven for 20 minutes, or until well risen and a skewer inserted into the middle of the cupcakes comes out clean. Leave to cool in the pans for 5 minutes before transferring to a wire rack to cool completely.

To make the meringue buttercream, put the sugar and egg whites in a heatproof bowl set over a pan of simmering water. Whisk until it reaches at least 60°C/140°F on a sugar thermometer. Pour into the bowl of a freestanding electric mixer fitted with the whisk attachment (or use an electric whisk and mixing bowl). Beat until the mixture has doubled in volume, cooled, and will stand in stiff, glossy peaks – this will take about 3 minutes.

Gradually add the butter to the cooled meringue mix, beating constantly, until the frosting is smooth. Fold in the vanilla and the strawberry jam/jelly. Spread the frosting over the cold cupcakes and arrange the summer berries on top of each one in a lovely cascade. Dust with icing/confectioners' sugar just before serving.

rosewater cupcakes

115 g/8 tablespoons butter,
at room temperature

115 g/½ cup plus
1 tablespoon caster/
granulated sugar

2 eggs

115 g/¾ cup plus
1 tablespoon self-raising/
rising flour

1 tablespoon rosewater

to decorate

12 pink rose petals

1 egg white, beaten

1 tablespoon caster/
superfine sugar

1½–2 tablespoons lemon
juice, as required

145 g/1 cup icing/
confectioners' sugar

pink food colouring

*a 12-hole muffin pan, lined
with paper cupcake cases*

makes 12

*Delicately scented with rosewater, these gorgeous pink
cupcakes are perfect for those who like things extra pretty.*

Preheat the oven to 180°C (350°F) Gas 4.

Beat the butter and sugar together in a bowl until pale and fluffy, then beat
in the eggs, one at a time. Sift the flour into the mixture and fold in, then
stir in the rosewater.

Spoon the mixture into the paper cases and bake for about 17 minutes
until risen and golden and a skewer inserted in the centre comes out clean.
Transfer to a wire rack to cool.

To decorate, brush each rose petal with egg white, then sprinkle with
caster/granulated sugar and leave to dry for about 1 hour.

Put 1½ tablespoons lemon juice in a bowl, then sift the icing/
confectioners' sugar into the bowl and stir until smooth. Add a little more
lemon juice as required to make a smooth icing. Add one or two drops of
food colouring to achieve a pale pink frosting, then drizzle over the cakes.
Top each one with a sugared rose petal. Leave to set before serving.

mini meringues

These tiny, pale pink meringues with their melt-in-the-mouth texture are ideal for any afternoon tea party. Serve them piled up on a plate – just as they are – or sandwich them together with whipped cream.

2 small or 1 large egg white

60 g/⅓ cup caster/
superfine sugar

a few drops of red food
colouring

whipped cream, to serve
(optional)

*2 baking sheets, covered with
parchment paper*

makes about 20

Preheat the oven to 110°C (225°F) Gas ¼.

Put the egg white in a clean, grease-free bowl and whisk until soft peaks form. Whisk in the sugar, one tablespoon at a time, until the meringue is thick and glossy. Add a few drops of red food colouring with the last tablespoon of sugar to achieve a pretty rose pink.

Dollop teaspoonfuls of the meringue mixture on the prepared baking sheets, spacing them well apart, and bake in the oven for about 1¼ hours until crisp. Turn off the oven and leave the meringues in the oven to cool. Serve plain or sandwiched together with a little whipped cream.

victoria sponge cake with fresh mint & strawberries

This classic cake is best eaten as fresh as possible. It is also delicious filled with good-quality raspberry jam/jelly and some whipped cream.

200 g/1 stick plus
6 tablespoons unsalted
butter, softened

200 g/1 cup caster/
granulated sugar

4 large eggs, lightly beaten

1 teaspoon vanilla extract

200 g/1²/₃ cups self-raising/
rising flour, sifted

2 teaspoons baking powder

a pinch of salt

icing/confectioners' sugar,
for dusting

filling

250 g/2¼ cups ripe
strawberries

2 tablespoons icing/
confectioners' sugar

grated zest of 1 lemon

150 g/²/₃ cup crème fraîche
or sour cream, chilled

100 g/½ cup mascarpone,
chilled

1 tablespoon shredded
mint leaves

*two 20-cm/8-in cake pans,
4 cm/1½ in deep, lightly
buttered and base-lined with
parchment paper*

serves 8

Preheat the oven to 180°C (350°F) Gas 4.

Put the butter and sugar in an electric mixer (or use a large mixing bowl and an electric whisk) and beat for 3–4 minutes, or until pale and fluffy. Gradually add the beaten eggs with the beaters still running, followed by the vanilla extract, flour, baking powder and salt. Mix until all the ingredients are combined.

Divide the mixture between the prepared pans and spread it evenly with a spatula. Bake in the oven for 25 minutes, or until lightly golden and risen. Leave to cool in the pans for 30 minutes. Tip the cakes out onto a wire rack and peel off the base papers. Leave to cool completely.

To make the filling, hull and thinly slice the strawberries, then mix in a bowl with half the icing/confectioners' sugar and all the lemon zest. Leave to macerate for up to 30 minutes.

In another bowl, use a balloon whisk to beat the crème fraîche and mascarpone together until smooth. Stir in the rest of the icing/confectioners' sugar and the shredded mint.

To assemble, place one cake on a board or large serving plate and spread the creamy filling over the top. Scatter the strawberries over the filling. Place the other cake on top and dust with icing/confectioners' sugar.

almond cake

225 g/1 cup plus
2 tablespoons caster sugar

150 g/1 stick plus
2 tablespoons butter, softened
and cubed

4 large eggs

1 teaspoon almond extract

75 g/scant $^2/_3$ cup self-raising/
rising flour

1 rounded teaspoon baking
powder

125 g/scant 1 cup ground
almonds

to finish

100 g/$^3/_4$ cup plus
1 tablespoon icing/
confectioners' sugar

freshly squeezed juice
of 1 small lemon

2 tablespoons toasted flaked/
slivered almonds

*an 18-cm/7-in round,
loose-based cake pan,
7 cm/3 in deep, lightly
buttered and base-lined
with parchment paper*

serves 8

*This is delicious eaten with baked rhubarb – cut some
rhubarb into chunks, sprinkle generously with sugar and
bake at the same temperature as the cake for 15–20 minutes.*

Preheat the oven to 180°C (350°F) Gas 4.

Put all the ingredients for the cake in an electric mixer (or use a large
mixing bowl and electric whisk) and beat until combined.

Pour the mixture into the prepared pan and spread it evenly with a spatula.
Put the pan on a baking sheet and bake in the oven for 40 minutes, or
until golden and firm to the touch in the centre. Leave the cake to cool
in the pan.

Tip the cold cake out of the pan and remove the parchment paper. Place
on a wire rack set over a board.

To finish, sift the icing/confectioners' sugar into a bowl and stir in the
lemon juice, little by little. You probably won't need it all – you are aiming
for a thick pouring icing. Spoon the icing over the cake, letting it drizzle
down the sides and scatter the flaked almonds on the top. Serve with the
baked rhubarb on the side.

marble cake

50 g/⅓ cup dark/bittersweet chocolate, chopped

175 g/1½ cups plain/all-purpose flour

1 generous teaspoon baking powder

175 g/1½ sticks unsalted butter, softened

200 g/1 cup caster/granulated sugar

4 eggs, lightly beaten

1 teaspoon vanilla extract

2 tablespoons milk

chocolate frosting
350 g/12 oz. dark/bittersweet chocolate, roughly chopped

225 g/2 sticks butter

225 ml/scant 1 cup milk

1 teaspoon vanilla extract

450 g/3⅓ cups icing/confectioners' sugar, sifted

chocolate sprinkles

Two 450-g/1-lb loaf pans, greased

serves 8–10

This recipe makes two smaller cakes – one to give as a gift and one to eat!

Preheat the oven to 180°C (350°F) Gas 4. Line the base and ends of each loaf pan with a strip of greased parchment paper.

Put the chocolate in a heatproof bowl over a pan of simmering water and stir until melted.

Put the butter and sugar in the bowl of an electric mixer and cream until pale and light. Gradually add the beaten eggs, mixing well between each addition and scraping down the sides of the bowl with a rubber spatula. Mix in the vanilla extract.

Sift the flour and baking powder together into a bowl. Tip the sifted flour and baking powder into the batter and mix until smooth. Stir in the milk. Spoon one-third of this mixture into the melted chocolate. Mix until smooth.

Drop alternate spoonfuls of vanilla and chocolate batter into one of the prepared loaf pans. When it's half full, give the pan a sharp tap on the work surface to

level the mixture. To create a marbled effect, drag the blade of a table knife through the mixture to create swirls. Do not over-swirl the mixture. Repeat this step with the second loaf pan.

Put the pans on the middle shelf of the oven. Bake for 40 minutes until a skewer inserted into the cakes comes out clean. Remove the pans from the oven. Leave to cool slightly before lifting the cakes onto a wire rack to cool.

To make the chocolate frosting, melt the chocolate and butter together in a heatproof bowl. Set over a pan of barely simmering water. Stir until melted and smooth, then set aside to cool.

In another bowl, beat the milk, vanilla and icing/confectioners' sugar until smooth. Add the cooled chocolate mixture and stir until smooth. Leave the frosting to thicken slightly before spreading over each cold cake, finishing with chocolate sprinkles.

white chocolate & apricot roulade

4 large eggs

100 g/½ cup caster/ granulated sugar

2 pinches of saffron threads

100 g/¾ cup self-raising/ rising flour, sifted

3 tablespoons flaked/ slivered almonds

1 tablespoon icing/confectioners' sugar, plus extra for dusting

apricot filling

seeds from 4 cardamom pods, crushed

1 tablespoon orange blossom honey or other clear honey

1 tablespoon freshly squeezed lemon juice

8 apricots, pitted and finely chopped

white chocolate cream

75 g/3 oz. white chocolate, broken into pieces

175 g/scant ⅔ cup crème fraiche or sour cream

200 ml/⅔ cup double/ heavy cream

a 24 x 37-cm/9– 14½-in Swiss/jelly roll pan, 2.5 cm/1 in deep, oiled and base-lined with parchment paper

serves 10–12

This summery roulade is pretty as a picture and makes a stunning centrepiece for any tea party.

Preheat the oven to 190°C (375°F) Gas 5.

Put the eggs, sugar and saffron in a heatproof bowl and place over a pan of simmering water. Using an electric whisk, beat the ingredients for 5 minutes until voluminous. Remove from the heat and fold in the flour.

Tip the mixture into the prepared pan and spread it evenly with a spatula. Sprinkle the almonds over the top. Bake for 12–15 minutes, until lightly golden. Cover a board with a sheet of parchment paper and a tablespoon of icing/confectioners' sugar.

When the cake is ready, leave it to settle, out of the oven, for 10 minutes. Run a sharp knife around the edges before turning it upside down over the parchment paper. Remove the pan and peel off the base paper. Roll up the cake from one of the shorter ends,

rolling the sugared parchment with it as you do so. Leave to cool.

To make the apricot filling, put all the ingredients in a saucepan and simmer, uncovered, for 10 minutes until the apricots are soft. Leave to cool, then refrigerate until needed.

To make the white chocolate cream, put the chocolate and 2 tablespoons of the crème fraiche in a heatproof bowl over a pan of barely simmering water. Leave until melted, stirring occasionally. Take the bowl off the heat and leave to cool slightly. Whisk the cream in a bowl until it forms soft peaks, then stir in the remaining crème fraiche and the cooled chocolate mixture.

Unroll the cake onto a board. Spread over the white chocolate cream, top with the apricot filling, and roll up the roulade. Dust with icing/confectioners' sugar.

rosewater, pistachio & grapefruit cake

200 g/1¼ cups shelled
pistachios

200 g/1⅔ cups self-raising/
rising flour

1 tablespoon bicarbonate
of soda/baking soda

150 g/1 stick plus 2
tablespoons butter, cubed

150 g/¾ cup caster/
granulated sugar

3 large eggs, lightly beaten

2 tablespoons rosewater

4 tablespoons buttermilk

grated zest of 2 grapefruit

a few crystallized rose petals,
to decorate

plain yogurt, to serve

grapefruit syrup

1 grapefruit

1 tablespoon rosewater

75 g/scant ½ cup
caster/superfine sugar

*a 23-cm/9-in springform cake
pan, 6 cm/2½ in deep, lightly
buttered*

serves 10–12

*This delicious and delicately-flavoured cake is perfect
decorated with pretty pink crystallized rose petals.*

Preheat the oven to 180°C (350°F) Gas 4.

Begin by whizzing 150 g/1 cup of the pistachios in a food processor until finely ground. Roughly chop the remaining 50 g/⅓ cup and mix three-quarters of them with the ground pistachios. Reserve the rest for scattering on the cake to decorate.

Sift the flour and bicarbonate of soda/baking soda into the bowl of an electric mixer. Add the butter and mix together, on the lowest speed, until the mixture resembles clumpy breadcrumbs. Add the pistachios, sugar, beaten eggs, rosewater, buttermilk and grapefruit zest and mix until combined.

Tip the mixture into the prepared cake pan and spread it evenly with a spatula. Bake in the oven for 45 minutes, or until golden and risen.

Towards the end of the cooking time, make the grapefruit syrup. Squeeze the juice of the grapefruit through a sieve/strainer and into a medium saucepan. Add the rosewater and sugar to the pan and gently heat together, stirring, until the sugar has dissolved. Increase the heat and boil for 2 minutes to make the liquid slightly more syrupy.

When the cake is ready, remove it from the oven and, using a small, fine skewer, make a few holes over the surface of the cake. Spoon over the warm grapefruit syrup, allowing it to seep in between spoonfuls. Leave the cake to cool completely in its pan.

Once cold, pop the cake out of the pan and scatter the reserved chopped pistachios and a few crystallized rose petals on top.

New York cheesecake

200 g/2 cups digestive biscuits/graham crackers or dark/bittersweet-chocolate cookies

60 g/4 tablespoons melted butter

1 kg/4 1/2 cups cream cheese

250 g/1 1/3 cup caster/superfine sugar

grated zest and juice of 1 lemon

200 ml/scant 1 cup sour cream

2 tablespoons vanilla extract

5 eggs

4 tablespoons plain/all purpose flour

a selection of fresh soft fruit

a springform cake pan, about 20 cm/4 in diameter

serves 8–10

This cheesecake is so rich and creamy that it really needs no embellishment. To make it extra special, simply smother the top with a selection of fresh soft fruit such as cherries, raspberries, strawberries or blueberries.

Preheat the oven to 140°C (275°F) Gas 1.

Crush the biscuits/cookies in a food processor then add the melted butter and mix well. Press the mixture firmly into the cake pan. Bake for 5 minutes, remove from the oven and let cool. Grease the sides of the pan above the crust.

In a large bowl, beat the cream cheese and sugar with an electric whisk. Add the lemon zest and juice, sour cream and vanilla extract. Mix until smooth and add the eggs one at a time until well combined. Put the flour in last and mix again. Pour the mixture into the cake pan.

Bake for 70 minutes until it is firm and the top is turning lightly golden. Let sit in the oven with the door open until cool (about 2 hours), then refrigerate for at least 6 hours or overnight. Place your favourite fresh fruit on top and serve dusted with icing/confectioners' sugar.

summer berry tartlets
with vanilla cream

*These pretty tartlets, filled with crème pâtissière and
topped with summer berries make perfect edible gifts.*

pastry

110 g/¾ cup plain/all-purpose
flour, plus extra for dusting

60 g/½ stick butter

30 g/2 tablespoons caster/
granulated sugar

1 egg yolk

a few drops of vanilla extract

crème pâtissière

1 tablespoon cornflour/
cornstarch

60 g/⅓ cup caster/
granulated sugar

1 egg and 1 egg yolk

100 ml/scant ½ cup milk

150 ml/⅔ cup double/
heavy cream

1 vanilla bean, split lengthwise

to assemble

200 g/1½ cups summer berries

3 tablespoons apricot preserve

juice of 2 small lemons

*a round fluted cutter
(6 cm/2½ in diameter)*

*24 mini tartlet tins/pans,
greased baking parchment*

baking beans

*a piping bag fitted with a round
nozzle/tip*

makes 24

To make the pastry, sift the flour into a mixing bowl and rub in the butter until the mixture resembles fine breadcrumbs. Add the sugar, egg yolk and vanilla and mix together to a soft dough with your fingers, adding a little cold water if the mixture is too dry. Wrap in plastic wrap and chill in the fridge for 1 hour.

Preheat the oven to 180°C (350°F) Gas 4. On a flour-dusted surface, roll out the pastry to a thickness of 3 mm/⅛ in. Stamp out 24 rounds using the cutter and press one into each hole in the pan, trimming away any excess pastry. Chill in the fridge for 30 minutes. Line each pastry case with parchment paper and fill with baking beans. Bake for 12–15 minutes, until golden brown and crisp. Leave to cool in the pans for 10 minutes, then transfer to a wire rack and leave to cool completely.

To prepare the crème pâtissière, whisk the cornflour/cornstarch, sugar, egg and egg yolk until creamy. Put the milk, cream and vanilla in a saucepan and bring to the boil. Pour in the egg mixture, whisking all the time. Return to the pan and cook for a few minutes until thick, then remove the vanilla bean. Pass through a sieve/strainer and set aside to cool.

Pipe the crème pâtissière into the pastry cases and top with berries. Heat the preserve and lemon juice in a saucepan then strain and brush over each tartlet to glaze.

vanilla & white chocolate babycakes

60 g/4 tablespoons butter,
at room temperature

60 g/scant ⅓ cup
caster/granulated sugar

1 egg, beaten

60 g/scant ½ cup self-raising/
rising flour

¼ teaspoon vanilla extract

1 tablespoon milk

to decorate

60 g/2½ oz. white chocolate,
chopped

green food colouring

pink food colouring

15 pastel-coloured candies

*a 12-hole mini muffin pan
or a baking sheet*

makes 12

For their sheer cuteness alone, these pastel-coloured mini cupcakes are absolutely irresistible. A perfect gift for a new mother to celebrate the arrival of her baby.

Preheat the oven to 180°C (350°F) Gas 4, then line the muffin pan with petit fours cases. (If you don't have a mini muffin pan, arrange the cases on a baking sheet; the cases should be able to cope with such a small amount of mixture.)

Beat the butter and sugar together in a bowl until pale and fluffy, then beat in the egg, a little at a time. Sift the flour into the mixture and fold in, then add the vanilla and milk and stir to combine.

Spoon the mixture into the paper cases, then bake for about 15 minutes until risen and golden and the tops spring back when gently pressed. Transfer to a wire rack to cool.

To decorate, divide the chocolate among three heatproof bowls and melt over a saucepan of simmering water or in a microwave. Leave to cool slightly, then stir a couple of drops of green food colouring into one bowl of chocolate and a couple of drops of pink into another. Leave the third bowl of chocolate plain.

Spoon white chocolate over four of the cakes, pink over another four and green over the remaining four, then top each one with a candy. Serve while the chocolate is still soft, or leave to set and package up as a gift.

little maids of honour

These traditional English tartlets are filled with almond paste and fruit preserve. Similar to bakewell tarts, they make an elegant gift.

pastry

110 g/³⁄₄ cup plus 2 tablespoons plain/all-purpose flour, plus extra for dusting

60 g/¹⁄₂ stick butter

30 g/2¹⁄₂ tablespoons caster/granulated sugar

1 egg yolk

filling

3 tablespoons lemon curd or other fruit preserve

3 tablespoons mascarpone

50 g/¹⁄₃ cup whole blanched almonds

50 g/1¹⁄₂ oz. sliced brioche or challah bread

60 g/¹⁄₂ stick butter, softened

2 tablespoons caster/superfine sugar

1 large egg

1 teaspoon vanilla extract

finely grated zest of 1 lemon

to decorate

24 whole blanched almond halves

icing/confectioners' sugar, for dusting

a 24-hole/cup mini muffin pan, greased

a flower-shaped cutter (6 cm/2¹⁄₂ in diameter)

a piping bag fitted with large round nozzle/tip

makes 24

To make the pastry, sift the flour into a mixing bowl and rub in the butter until the mixture resembles fine breadcrumbs. Add the sugar and egg yolk and mix together to form a soft dough with your fingertips, adding a little cold water if the mixture is too dry. Wrap in plastic wrap and chill in the fridge for 1 hour.

Preheat the oven 180°C (350°F) Gas 4. On a flour-dusted surface, roll out the pastry to a thickness of 3 mm/¹⁄₈ in. Stamp out 24 flower shapes with the cutter and put one flower in each hole of the muffin pan, pressing them against the base and side of the pan. Chill in the fridge until needed.

Put ¹⁄₃ teaspoon each of lemon curd and mascarpone in the bottom of each pastry case. Put the almonds and brioche in a blender and blitz to a fine crumb. Cream together the butter and sugar, then add the egg, vanilla, lemon zest and almond mixture. Mix everything well and then spoon into the piping bag. Pipe a small amount of filling into each tartlet case to fill. Top each one with an almond half and bake for 12–15 minutes, until golden brown. Dust with icing/confectioners' sugar and serve warm or cold.

almond praline macarons

Caramel is delicious in all its forms, and when mixed with almonds, it's a match made in heaven. Add whipped cream and you've got yourself a very delicious macaron.

basic macarons

200 g/1½ cups icing/
confectioners' sugar

100 g/⅔ cup ground almonds

120–125 g/½ cup egg whites
(about 3 eggs)

a pinch of salt

40 g/3 tablespoons caster/
superfine sugar

2 tablespoons flaked/slivered
almonds, chopped

1 tablespoon icing/
confectioners' sugar

filling

50 g/⅓ cup blanched almonds

50 g/¼ cup caster/
superfine sugar

125 ml/½ cup double/
heavy cream

3 solid baking sheets

makes about 20

Prepare the filling before you make the macaron shells. Preheat the oven to 180°C (350°F) Gas 4. Line 2 of the baking sheets with parchment paper and oil the third sheet with sunflower oil.

Tip the blanched almonds into a small roasting pan and toast in the oven for about 5 minutes. Leave to cool slightly.

Put the sugar and 1 tablespoon water in a saucepan over low–medium heat and let the sugar dissolve completely. Increase the heat and bring to the boil, then cook until the syrup turns to an amber-coloured caramel. Add the toasted almonds to the pan and, working quickly, stir to coat in the caramel. Tip the praline mixture onto the oiled baking sheet and leave until completely cold. Break the cold, hard praline into pieces and whizz in the food processor until finely ground. Store in an airtight container until ready to use.

Prepare the Basic Macarons according to the recipe on page 24.

Pipe rounds of mixture onto the lined baking sheets. Tap the baking sheets sharply on the work surface, then scatter the chopped slivered almonds and icing/confectioners' sugar over the tops. Leave the macarons to rest for 15 minutes–1 hour.

Preheat the oven to 170°C (325°F) Gas 3.

Bake the macarons on the middle shelf of the preheated oven, one sheet at a time, for 10 minutes. Leave to cool on the baking sheet. Lightly whip the cream and stir in the ground praline. Spread the filling over half the macaron shells and sandwich with the other half. Leave to rest for 30 minutes before packaging.

prune, cinnamon & toasted walnut cookies with cinnamon icing

75 g/³⁄₄ cup walnut pieces

100 g/7 tablespoons butter, softened

150 g/²⁄₃ cup light brown soft sugar

1 large egg, lightly beaten

2 tablespoons cream cheese

75 g/scant ²⁄₃ cup light brown and 75 g/scant ²⁄₃ cup white self-raising/rising flour

2 teaspoons ground cinnamon

a pinch of salt

125 g/²⁄₃ cup pitted, soft Agen prunes, snipped into small pieces

cinnamon icing
50 g/¹⁄₃ cup icing/confectioners' sugar

2–3 pinches of ground cinnamon

2 baking sheets, oiled

makes about 20

These delicious spiced cookies can be made even more decadent by substituting half the water in the icing with Armagnac for a more indulgent flavour.

Preheat the oven to 200°C (400°F) Gas 6.

Spread the walnuts on a baking sheet and toast in the preheated oven for 5 minutes, then leave to cool.

Put the butter and sugar in an electric mixer (or use a large mixing bowl and an electric whisk) and beat until light and fluffy. Add the egg and cream cheese and mix again to combine. Sift in the flours (add any bran left in the sieve/strainer from the brown flour, if using), the cinnamon and salt and mix again. Fold in the toasted walnuts and the prunes with a large metal spoon.

Drop craggy mounds of the mixture onto the prepared baking sheets – about 1 generous dessertspoonful each. Leave room between them to allow the cookies to spread as they bake; 6 or 7 per baking sheet is about right, so you will need to cook them in batches. Bake the cookies in the oven for 10–12 minutes, or until golden. Leave to cool for a few minutes, then transfer to a wire rack to cool completely.

To make the cinnamon icing, sift the icing/confectioners' sugar and cinnamon into a small bowl. Add 2 teaspoons cold water and mix – adding a few more drops of water if needed. Drizzle a little icing over each cookie and leave to set.

mint chocolate kisses

175 g/1 cup dark/bittersweet chocolate, chopped

175 g /1½ sticks unsalted butter

2 medium eggs

225 g/1 cup plus 2 tablespoons packed light brown soft sugar

250 g/2 cups self-raising/ rising flour

¾ teaspoon baking powder

a pinch of salt

minty buttercream

75 g/5 tablespoons unsalted butter, softened

150 g/1 cup icing/ confectioners' sugar, sifted

½–1 teaspoon peppermint extract, to decorate

200 g/7 oz. dark/ bittersweet chocolate, chopped

sugar sprinkles, to decorate

2 baking sheets, lined with baking parchment

makes about 18

This is the kind of treat to put a smile on anyone's face – it has something to do with the nostalgic combination of chocolate and mint topped with pretty sugar sprinkles.

Put the chocolate and butter in a heatproof bowl set over a pan of barely simmering water. Stir until smooth and thoroughly combined.

Put the eggs and sugar in the bowl of a freestanding electric mixer fitted with the whisk attachment (or use an electric whisk and mixing bowl) and beat until pale and light. Add the chocolate mixture and mix until smooth.

Sift together the flour, baking powder and salt. Add to the mixing bowl and stir until smooth. Bring together into a dough, cover and refrigerate for a couple of hours.

When you are ready to start baking, preheat the oven to 180°C (350°F) Gas 4.

Remove the dough from the fridge and pull off walnut-size pieces. Roll into balls and arrange on the prepared baking sheets. Bake in batches on the middle shelf of the oven for about 12 minutes, or until

the cookies are crisp on the edges but slightly soft in the middle. Leave to cool on the sheets for a few minutes before transferring to a wire rack to cool completely.

To make the minty buttercream, put the butter in a large bowl and, using a freestanding mixer or electric whisk, cream until really soft. Gradually add the sifted icing/ confectioners' sugar and beat until pale and smooth. Add peppermint extract to taste.

Sandwich the cold cookies together with the minty buttercream.

To decorate, put the chocolate in a heatproof bowl set over a pan of barely simmering water. Stir until smooth and melted. Leave to cool slightly. Half-dip the cookies in the melted chocolate, scatter with sugar sprinkles and leave on baking parchment to set before packaging.

index

picture credits

Martin Brigdale pages 33, 37, 38, 55

Peter Cassidy page 10

Laura Edwards pages 2–3, 30

Tara Fisher pages 6, 22

Jonathan Gregson pages 9, 13, 14, 21

Richard Jung page 18

William Lingwood pages 5, 7, 51, 52, 56, 64

Lisa Linder page 44

William Reavell page 4

Kate Whitaker endpapers, pages 1, 8, 17, 23, 25, 26, 29, 34, 40, 41, 43, 47, 48, 53, 59, 60, 63

recipe credits

Tonia George pages 8, 12, 15, 20

Isidora Popovic page 11

Linda Collister page 19

Annie Rigg pages 23, 24, 27, 28, 31, 35, 45, 50, 58, 62

Susannah Blake pages 32, 36, 39, 54

Sarah Randell pages 16, 41, 42, 46, 49, 61

Hannah Miles pages 53, 57